The Afternoon in Dismay

The Afternoon in Dismay

by Peter Wild

Acknowledgments: *American Weave; Ananke; Burning Water; Cranium Press; December Magazine; Epoch; Experiment; From a Window; Goliards; The Green World; Hollow Orange; Intermission Magazine-Chicago; Kayak; Poet and Critic; Poetry Dial; Polygon Press; Prairie Schooner; Scimitar and Song; Southern Poetry Review; Sprarrow Magazine; Today; Wormwood Review; Writer's Digest.*

Poetry Editor, Dallas E. Wiebe
Published by the Art Association of Cincinnati, Inc. 1968
Drawings, design and typography by Noel Martin

Contents

Afternoon

Those faded eyes of a broken artist,
how they watch the afternoon in dismay!
                                        —Lorca

So lacking in talent
but not wisdom,
he went far off
down the beach;
made a home
on a pile of rocks.
and spent his time
from then on learning
to sleep passive
beneath the moon,
how to sit patient
in the sun. . .

but often, while picking
*   dully at crab meat*
broken fresh from the shell,
*   caught himself playing*
imaginary games
*   with the pelicans.*

Ram

Insistent pain behind the eyes announces
the turning solstice, the coming of spring;
gambit for marbles, season of weddings:
time for exams. my sinuses protest
the marching of the Ram, too slow the body
swings listless; marble muscles
cry repose, while a fermented grain
tears and grumbles in the dozing bowels.

but the good will know in their veins the time
to move for the proof of their ethic; the bad
flounder with broken forelegs in the receding
riptide of their dreams. I straddle the fence,
see dying moths in an old man's eyes, squirming
hooks of sperm in the genitals of a sleeping youth.

Watchman

Wooden tongues do not eat up my silence,
this night shot smooth with bolts, and a yard
of unchained dogs; goats sleep,
and all around the village stout bars
thump into place behind heavy doors.
the moon wobbles over the haystacks
like a virgin boy into a wilderness franchise:
my cabbage mind sprouts leaves of silver.

peg-legged old man, pass by, freeze—
wander drunken into the forest where wolves
will make you human in their bowels. but
at the corner I hear his clapper, the moist cough:
bolts twist in the buckling jamb,
dogs nibble on slices of the moon.

Magdalena

Banded in brass a smiling cock rears up
over the mountains, crisscrossed
with dark oaks and patches of snow.
when the breath of dogs has frozen
in their lungs, and all the doors are locked.
he has the key to the moon in his pocket
and carries a scalpstick strung with skulls.
he lays his chin between the steeples
of the whitewashed church (the bones
rumble in their urn) and leers
down into the plaza filled with ghosts
of blossoms and counting girls.

he ignores the blood-smeared doors
and pierces armpits to their heart root.

Consuelo of the moon

Consuelo
carries green melons
beneath the cold moon.
the crickets in her hair
the serpent at her feet

she walks across
the newly-plowed earth,
the snow on the mountains
is hardly breathing:
from underneath the stones
beetles watch her
with huge eyes,
and in their nests
the birds talk in their sleep
as they dream

the snowfrost hangs low
in the contours of the earth
and her breath
turns to little puffs of frost

Consuelo carries
green melons.
the snake
slithers quietly
into the brook
and the crickets
are nuggets of gold

she carries
green melons
across the newly-plowed earth

The marvelous dog

Across the steppes
comes the dog full of holes

in his mouth he carries
a salami sandwich;
on his head he wears
a crown of white onions

in the pouch around his shoulder
is a flask of clear vinegar

he is carrying in it
messages for his lady

to put on her face
to put on her hands.

he sees the sharp stars
moveless above him,
even now the
cherries burn in his eyes

as he runs with dusty paws,
smiling, and running faster. . .

he is bringing
messages for his glass lady
of clear vinegar

to put on her face
to put on her hands

and onions
to put in her eyes

El pez de la noche

The fish of the night
carries a yellow lantern in his mouth.
his tail is made of a sickle.
his stomach is full
of sleeping men and women

he floats down alleys
and the rabbits kick in their dreams,
he glides down the street
and bumps his nose against the windows:

the fish of the night
wears a joker's cap hung with tin bells
and a fat monk's belt around his girth.
he lifts a leg to pee on the corner of a building:
and waking in the middle of the night
you can smell his stale breath as he passes
in search of fenders and empty bottles.

3 poems

I.

The crickets watch you,
                    María,
in your crib.

they watch you.

the hills lie covered
in lambs' fleece,
and four jaundiced horses
tear at their halters.

they are waiting for the balloonman
to pass barefoot through the snow.
see the blood
he leaves in his tracks!

and for the droplets of water
in which they can see their reflection,
the words to restore
tongues to their mouths.

with their huge eyes,
the crickets watch you,
                    María,
and dangle emblems of frogs
        over the crib rail.

II.

the rain is looking for your eye,
                              María,
to find a pock
      in which to test itself.

to run its mettle
      against its own mettle in spite.

the small boy goes from
                     door to door
with a cupful of lilies;
only later do they find
his thumbprint on their eyeballs;

while in the rushes
      an old crocodile
cannot find his tears,
but through his fiery sockets
crawls a salamander,

with a fist of nails
to plant in the brow of the storm.

III.

and now that the sand
  has had its way with you,
rasping the flesh
  from your innocent bone. . .

flesh of sand.

the finger of wind
  pointed at you:
and now a river of cities
  runs between your legs. . .

cities of wind.

you did not know that your breasts,
  bitten by spiders,
would smother the babes of the world
  with flowers. . .

flowers of death.

or that the fish sleeping
  on your ignorant brow
would leap through your crown
  to punish the air.

6 songs for Epiphany

The coffee dog

The coffee dog
sat in the stream.
he came with the intent
          of catching fishes,
but instead watched
the chocolate birds
building nests
          of rhinestone crosses,
and was content to spend the afternoon
               with the icy water
cooling his bottom

The storm fox

The storm fox
        has set his sails,
he has tapped his lines
and crosshatched the diamond rock.
not even the forest ranger knows
where the artful traps
                with their delectable meats
and black berries
are set

let the jaws snap
        where the foot falls.

he crouches low in the grove
and with lightning in his eyes
        watches the storm clouds
come up,

between his paws
        he rolls the cold dice
of a badger's eyes

The lucky hedgehog

The lucky hedgehog
went looking for jackstones
           of gold
and found his feet
    buried in green buckeyes

in the full moon
    he went through the cornfields
where he had heard
    there were little girls swinging
in half loops of silver;

being myopic, he pointed
    his nose to the moon,
for the most part expecting
    only sticks and mud
or a few tasteless mussels

but from the sky fell
    a fireworks of appleblossoms
and at his feet he found
    the ground covered with buckeyes

The happy alligator

The happy alligator
with the triangular tongue
he was very happy
because all day long
he'd been feeding on mosquitoes

and now with his chin
in the reddening water
    had climbed with limp feet
      up the rungs of words

and with his head stuck
    into the heart of a mango
he dreamt of feeding
    on the thousand lights
of an avocado

The electric bird

The electric bird
doesn't know
    that the flesh
has been stripped from his face

he only has
    that uncomfortable feeling
of Christmas lights
blinking in the sockets of his eyes

The wintergreen penguins

The wintergreen penguins
sweep the forest floor
with their wooden brooms

they tumble down the hills
concentrating
          on spokes.

and when the mortar
                goes off

they scramble back to their houses,
get dressed in their
          very best clothes,
and go to the wedding
     smelling of moth balls.

from Aragon

Aragon

It is easy to see
the birds have nothing to say
except to direct with glass batons
the firetrucks of gamblers
to Sunday conflagrations;

and tease the eyes
of dead Indians
recording star-crawls
on the brittle film
of their frigid gaze

(in the streets bloated crocodiles
will never catch up with their theses.)

Oleo struts

Everyone, even scholars,
            know
that at seven o'clock
    iron-headed dogs
are out catching dwarf stars
    by the nape of the neck,
and beat the straw out of them
            against anchored railings.

and the little girl angels
            come down
    in their sheer petticoats,
holding petits fours in their hands,
and fluttering in mid air
    hang colored ornaments
        in the bamboo grove.

while all the housewives
            and Mexicans
and groceryboys
        are running home.

Pico della

with corncob pipes
        and fish nets
we were trying to catch
              black Indians,
     newts
        and pearls
in the twilight

wading up to our knees
        in the pink surf
heard a locomotive,
but straining on the tackle
     found only a biting grisette
struggling in the meshes.

Brown moon

A brown moon rides upon the gulf
and a vast bay horse slips off the mountains
to paw the grass and feed on his reflection.

the distended city shivers in its bones
along the shore, rattles its teeth;
                              with pretty fingers
girls pull shawls over naked shoulders.

she rises tall from the distance of receding
plateaus, covered with burlap and dun armor.
oiled wheels turn slowly in her.

spoons sift water. the boat pivots slowly,
                              caught
in the field of a refracted promontory.
a herd of cartilaginous horses skitters on the plain.

luna lunera, dile que tenga compasión.

28

Charcoal

Wolves feed on the hind-
quarters of the moon,
above a windy chaos of fire,
air, earth and water

while a see of bishops
armed with burnt holly
files along the basalt foothills
of impending mountains.

dogs sleep. babies toss
in their cribs, dreaming of birds,
while chickens observe the horizon
with snake eyes. eggs stir.

on rice paper wings
an enormous cat floats
down from the tropical sea
to scratch in the sand.

Music for an aged and melancholy king

He thinks of black forests

> *and vultures*
> *soaring white*
> > *like drugged angels;*

he looks down the runways
> *of the sea*
and blows his glass trumpet
loud above the sea stones.

and pleasantly fatigued
> *beyond vulgar cities*
> > *discovers a maiden*

with transparent hair
> *and sequined slippers,*
who offers
> *all necessary secrets.*

now sleep, oh king,
> *clutching your nosegay*
> *in a pale fever.*

Colima

Suddenly
she jumped out before me
from behind a potter's stall
and ripped open her dress

on her breast lay
*   a glass pendant*
writhing in the sun like a snake.

and in it I saw
*   a long path*
lined with cool dark trees,
and fires burning
*   far out on the ocean;*
and heard the waves
*   like happy soldiers*
stumbling onto the shore

she was gone.
around me the peasants
*   were still bickering,*
and the sun cut into my head.

Poem of the virgin selling eggs

She came through the village
            on a Sunday,
barefoot and jeweled,
        selling eggs,
ringing a branch of bells,
her breasts exposed. . .

she came to the village
            from over the campos.
in peaked hat
            and thick glasses
looking like a teacher.

and smiling like a nun
                sold eggs
to the children.
        went away
down rows of dusty tamarisks. . .

we marveled
        that night
at the rain;
        and the little snakes
that broke out of the leathery eggs.

Pelicans

Bug-eyed
     they watch me swim,
a man
     without fins or webbed feet;
an object of suspicion.

strut flatfooted
     on their ramparts
or half doze
     or paddle innocently about
in little schools

but always keeping me
     in the corner of one eye,
as if reluctant to admit
     a man bears watching.

and finally, as I get closer,
     ruffle their feathers,
shift from foot to foot, and
     unable to bear it any longer

flap clumsily into the air,
     flying away with their
          secrets

leaving me to bob,
     a man alone and laughing
          in the water.

Mailman

When the mailman comes
lugging his leather pouch
of sticks and coals.

a beat-up man
in a baggy shirt,
but whistling

through packs of dogs
which help themselves
to chunks of his legs. . .

we hang from the doorways, dumb
as nuns about to behold
a spectacle of blood;

but confronted
by the rows of boxes,
he hesitates,

turns to show us
his burnt-out eyes,
a finger laid
along the side of his nose. . .

then smiling,
slips our little sins
one by one
into their slots.

Meridian

Around the sun
is a ring of turtles
a ruff of Milanese silk

a collar of evergreen
and a necklace of pearls
hard as steel.

leaning on his staff
he fingers absentmindedly
the bullets of his bandolier

and watches as bugles blast across the valley
and riders in grass capes post
through the orchards bearing messages
sealed with hemlock and cinnamon hearts

while in a stream of darts
blackbirds escape from his mouth.

An apology for wolves

I.

They have always
vilified us,
sensing our stealth
and their lack of it,

and moved by the first impulse
of their dim minds,
throw stones, beat shields,
catch us in their iron sights. . .

as if we wanted their women
or would steal their Gods. . .

II.

it is true, we've been caught
on occasion with the remnants
of petticoats still in our mouths,
or sporting a red cap, just for a lark.

but we've got a bad press
which capitalizes on such exceptions:
a grandmother or two
coughed up now and then,

and doesn't consider
our loss of face
when driven into the suburbs
by a long winter and heavy snows.

III.

actually, it's just a simple lack
of understanding—on their part,
a myopia common
to all muscular animals. . .

we mean no harm
but must pursue
that fine exhilaration
instinctively ours:

flaming tails in bushes
and leaves slipping along our backs.

3 poems for Silvia

I.

You fell from the arms
  of a furious angel
with black icicles on his brow,
which ripped across an old flood plain
      setting fire to the chaparral,
turning burros to charcoal
      where they stood. . .

fell wide-eyed
  with a spike in your head
into the ashes of your own soul.

II.

from a history
  of candles

and spearpoints
    twisted on themselves
to suck vitality
    from each others' necks,
and raised by their own poison
        fell
like bitten stars, pale
      with venom,
nameless under hooves.

from a sex
    that knew itself
in mud
  as only dumb.

III.

and if the sex of the child
    could be known—
that head split by lightning
    and dragged down by a winter beard—

it would be earth

    shooting sparks
into the burlap frame that holds it;

            new tendrils
curling from the wooden pores
        to test their mettle
            against the new white moon.

Tongues

The wind blows through the window
and fills the room,
freshens the bowl of flowers;
the sun glances on the deep varnish
of the furniture, strikes
the white sheets of the bed

shirtless,
I stand at the window
watching the city oxidize,
still and pink between
the quiet river and the sky;
as if perhaps in a hundred years
it will grow a tongue
and speak the words
to be remembered forever as holy:

you lie on the bed,
covers thrown back,
half stirred by light and wind;
also waiting for the kiss
to break you into day,

in your small mouth the tongue
struggles again and again
to form words which have no vowels
except those given by sunlight and wind.

The aluminum dog

He comes loping across the burning field,
vest filled with thermit grenades,

leaping his monocycle through
the blue flames of multiple hoops

(having ridden for months
through the tentacles of spring tides,
past lovesick boats
stuck in the mud),

and drawing up (the bullets of his bandoliers
sting in the sun), knocks down his kickstand,

rolls a cigarette, and holding his typewriter
in one hand, records our testimonies

while standing on one leg. see how
his handsome fangs protrude.

The virgin of Guaymas

I.

The virgin of Guaymas
lies in the sand,
clustered with chokeberries.
a bird clasped in her hand,
eyelids crusted with gold,
she does not hear the circling cries
as she sleeps, sweating in the sun.

II.

born from a rush of wind
she comes down the highway,
a leather bag stored with hours,
an armload of morning flowers;
walking in loose sandals over the backs
of fish, steadies her coronal
as she squints into overlapped horizons

III.

buoyed by haloes and streamers,
down streets lined with frogs,
her hands have lost their fingers
her feet turned to clay;
and spinning on her plexus
sees the indelible stain of an asp
smiling on her breast

IV.

in the provisional dawn, hand
crossed with spiders and crabs, she rolls
with the taste of nickels in her mouth;
the eaves dripping as she passes,
walks barefoot over cold sand,
wearing the garments of one
just risen from the grave

V.

she cannot hold the gray hoops
which circle her head. nor
the birds which blink in her eyes.
one ear torn off, barracuda
escape from her thighs.
although her hair is full of lights
her armpits smell of burnt powder.

To jump

Everything matters now
as I count them, pinching each in my memory
as a shepherd thumbs his time
stringing numbers to knots for company.

and if I had wanted,
I could know better:
for me they are strung with nothing more
than innumerable cigarettes
                    holding my nerve together,

until the arresting slap
locks us in our training
                    and we crowd patient to the door,

dropping each by each through his life
into the war.

Singing prince

Here I sit on my mat
before a basket of colored eggs,
playing my mandolin,
naked except for a crown

here surrounded by sand
and the stark walls of a blue sky,
I play, mindless of faces
which appear in the creosote.

I feel the wind on my ribs,
the sun on my stubble;
the sky is filled with yellow birds
and a fox comes, wagging his tail. . .

and at night when the mountains sink,
I stretch out, head on arm,
and sleep the dreams of ice cold water
sealed in ancient pottery.

To Linda

Holding hands, we suspected
bears in the woods:
grievous golden bears
would haunt us from the trees,
overstuffed probate bears
thumping their temples
and shaking their heads;
we saw undernourished Teddy bears
swinging through the trees
                    like children,
and polar bears.

and having no sense for the knack
of a Hansel and Gretel,
left ourselves
              to go
through the dark woods
                    alone.

Horse with an apron

Lord, he ran up the bolts of calico
        puffing like a locomotive
and disappeared in the aura of the court.
There was a commotion
        of shrieks and giggles,
bare feet running over marbles:
    out of the clouds
a voice bassooned
      "you're it."

and then reappeared, charging down
        cobblestones on the other side,
puffing even harder,
        but grinning and wiping his hands
on his polka-dotted apron.

On zebras

All day long I've been thinking of zebras.
how they hold vanilla ice cream cones
                    up over the battlements,
smiling like an Oriental ambassador
                    who has the upper hand,
but really doesn't give a damn
                    because he could blow you all
to smithereens if he wanted to.
but that isn't like a zebra.
they are more disposed to nosing
in the punch bowl for chunks of pineapple,
and when discovered
                    take a last quick gulp
                               bow,
and switching their tails
                    trot off whistling
before the hostess can call the butler.
but they do that just to tease.
more often zebras are to be found
lounging nonchalantly behind the arbors,
homemade wreaths about their necks,
                    meerschaums stuck in their vests,
feet propped up
                    reading the National Geographic;
and dropping cold pearls
                    into the ears of lovers,
excuse themselves with a slight cough
                    before their presence becomes indiscreet.
however, zebras are more partial
             to riding on the backs of submarines
or bounding down the streets
                    at six a.m. to wake the chickens,
and still more often you can see them
                    rolling the hoop of the moon
through the seasick sky

Ave

Above the vineyards
the angels circle,
heads massed
with tight curls of ram.

carrying in their horns
the myrrh of the angelus.
their eyes shine
the humor of the ox.

laughing, their skirts have become tangled
in the length of their swords;
and dive, kicking their feet
to set their legs free:

but across the fields they see
the red leopards running.
they feel cold hands
on the soles of their feet.

and raising their goblets
in a last toast of gall,
refract the prayers of the village
into the Hail Mary of the sun.

Sunday afternoon

We walk down the path,
the field mice
hide under brown leaves.

while up ahead in a maple grove
eleven golden horses
stand watching us,

Whiffs of gunpowder
swirling in the baskets of their heads,
amethyst moths
fluttering in their eyes.

Summer House

They spent their summer then
in a little town in Mexico
            hardly on the map
and impossible to pronounce.
in a little house down
the beach from the village,
shaded by banana trees —
really quite in luxury
(he had withdrawn all his money,
while her share came from
her father's account)
with a screened porch where
in the morning after sleeping late
he could prop his feet up on the
railing and smoke and listen to her
moving behind him in the house,
and watch the pelicans bobbing out
on the sea. and she was as satisfied
as perhaps she ever would be (except
for the occasional scorpions)

and spent the afternoons
lying side by side in the water,
jostled by the waves.

and when the time came,
picked themselves up and went
straight north,

she to get her master's
at a famous university,
he to dream of the pelicans
and the sound of her moving
behind in the house.

Cananea

I.

In her arms she holds
a tarbaby clustered with jewels,
with rubies and green snake eyes
of serpentine. about her shoulders
a lappet, purple as snow,
pinned with tiny hearts
stolen from the nests of crows.

around her head a crown of saltbush,
her cheeks are soft as gold.

her lips are crusted with froth
and in his fat hands he clutches
                              riverstones.

II.

at night she blunders across
the dark canyons carrying
a bundle of straw and telephone poles.

see the entrails she pulls
across the black snow.

comes barefoot off the mountainsides
into the white teeth of morning;
her breasts stand out
purple with cold.

burros choke,
donkeys cover their eyes.

as she passes through the hanged man's arch
houses rear back from the street,
the pavement buckles, churches
shiver and rattle their chains

in the garden her sisters
lie brittle in their dreams.

and pours out at the feet of mules
her basket of needles and beans,
while vested in his ermine maniple
he squats atop the mule-king's back

whispering into ribbed ears
learned jokes, vernal schemes.

III.

swollen by the dust of summer
she sits atop the slag heaps,
wearing a crown of onions and mud,
a coat riddled with holes.

and holding in her arms
a wooden doll sprouting spadices,
gives birth to a stream
of transparent ponies
which tumble, laughing, down the slopes.

beneath her in the plaza, horses go crazy
from eating lemons off the trees,
little girls tear up their skirts
while boys do handstands around them,
blowing on their plastic horns.

across the dusty arroyos, behind
the canyons, echo their thin whinnies.

Haystacks

Across the plains they slump
one behind the other,
backs to the moon;
chins sunk to breastplates
lances pointed to the ground

astride horses which have forgotten
the command to move on.

sleeping in their armor,
                    they themselves
cannot recall what the word was

once it passed through their minds
              like a wandering moth,
but disappeared
          before they could grasp it,

and now on their backs they can feel
                          only vaguely
slender fingers caressing metal,
the damp air
          eating into their joints

Caboose

Between once before my toes I saw
close where two thighs met like hills
a new taste to the touch of fingers,
miraculous, as never before among
the folds of the earth excreted. but here
in the last light behind eyelids
of granite sealed by refusal
to press the forefinger more to the blade —
here I saw as the caboose was a period,
a sprig
      of what
           in a glass
               only
                   to drink
is gone: boiling isinglass
                   never
                      cooled
or hammered to any Nordic's sword —
like the flaming one the performer swallows —
but this one left burnt salt behind.
and to look back on the city was
to take the sponge and squeeze it dry again:
squandering pebbles in my mouth (my tongue sticks still)

      take me home.
           I thought I said.
                 to take me home.

if one lives by the sea long enough,
he no longer hears the waves, and what
they've said is gossip fit for sewers.

When I get drunk again.
                        don't bother.
                                    taking me.

home.
            leave me sleep here.
                        where it's cold.
                                    and caboose.

Flojo

the afternoon has on long canvas pants
dissolving into sand, and all the quick peacock
eyes we saw watching us this morning
have ascended into the aqueous sky,
and lost their sight.
              the swollen head of midday
is slowly boiling
          with chunks of spicy meat.
I haven't got the purpose
                    to tie my shoes—
What would the afternoon care
                as it regards us through heavy lids. . . ?

if someone would go catch my horse
      who is feeding on the green moss of the river
and put some sour mash between his teeth,
if someone would beat the clouds
                    with a stick
so children and utter consequences
                        would fall.
and the lava hills
          sleeping like dumb black animals
would shake loose the white crosses,
                    spears in their flesh,

and yawning, open up to receive them
in their bosoms and heavy arms.

4 Cities of Padre Kino

San Ignacio

a great egg
        dominates
the horizon,
            pure chalk
wrested supreme
            from raw sand
and nails.

and from its turrets
        as from a sacred mountain,
the valley burns
        through the frigid afternoon
like lava through basalt and ice;
the flames of the trees
        and the dull tongues of the river
lick around its alabaster heels

and the dome
        remains aloof
            in its dimension
among blunted fires.

Magdalena

rid of flesh
  he stares up at star scrawls
    in the midnight sky;
his sockets
  are cold streets
rutted by winter rains.

listening to footsteps
  above him on the flags,
he clutches a brace of rotted pistols,
  a cross crumbling green
    on his yellow breast,
and remembers the wind
    like fire through his hair,
  the backs of the Indians
    and the wood squeezed to steel. . .

the stars accuse him
  windy days make him restless:
he gropes
  for his fingerprints
    in the dust;

and reaches out
  with broken hands
to catch the girls' skirts
    as they pass by.

Tubutama

a white cock
        gluts himself
on shattered rock
        and cactus,
and prunes himself
    to kiss the hen.

on a hilltop
    she sits across the lake,
blue-eyed
        and unanxious,
unaware of the slivers
    she accepts in her mouth;

though the earth tumbles
        beneath her
    and the sky tear with a scream;
mornings the plaza
        is trampled with splayed hooves
and the afternoon pinched
        by the clashing edges of suns,

unaware of herself,
    blue-eyed
        she accepts them into her breast,
and keeps her hilltop
        her quiet celebrations.

Caborca

Caborca sleeps
with its mouth full of glass eyes
its head
stinging with spines,
which keep watch on its intestines
and survey the probes
in its numb ears.

nobody knows
the words written on the slate thighs
of the mountains,
that lie exposed
and sentient to the midday —
they were put there by the finger
of an impotent king
and a torrent of horsetails
washed the sight
and meaning from their eyes. . .

they stand with glottises
paralyzed by a lean sun
and a fat moon
and await the dust
to choke up salvation
from their septic throats.

Desert

1.

Here all is intellect:
nothing escapes
            the omniscience
of a cruel god.

2.

shadows,
      event of his absence,
are not soft,
            but utterly vacant.

3.

bare sticks writhe up
            through the sand
into wavering heat;
thorns drive out
            of the wood
to whet themselves
            on the constant blaze.

4.

even the beaded animals
      walk

                  with fire
in their cast iron skulls.

5.

mountains crack
      to take the sky by the arms,
rocks split open
            to receive the spines
in their mouths.

6.

and at night,
   complete absence,

lave their sores
in the wash of the moon.

Spigots

Ants tickle the convolutions
in the nut of his head

(nutrified by cattails
and circumscription of melon)

the snow lies on his forearms
like the fleece of a lamb.

with visor down,
   waving his concrete sword,
he stands and laughs in the stirrups,

and rides his armor-plated horse
through a pleurisy of stars

steeply for the spigot of the moon.

Poinsettia

Across the windows
the little horses run
the moon in their eyes

they wear satin capes
and their throats
are made of silver.

in their mouths
is the taste
of cold green nickels

and in the wind they hear
a thousand
nickel bells.

they run faster
looking for them
in the wind,

across the windows
over the earth
strewn with glass.

with their noses
in the wind
the little horses run

forever and forever

to find the cold pasture
where the grass grows in the moon.

Poema por mi doncella

Up in the orange trees
   the crickets are singing,
among the dull stars of fruit
      which have long lost their points,
         and wait
            to fall in the morning

across the orchard
   the fragance of broken cloves —
      a thousand dead saints
who have risen from the ditches
   and wander blind through the fields

hidden in the cactus a coyote
      yaps sharply
         once to the moon.

the desert lies
   a huge sleeping dog
while the black cat of the mountains
            stands immobile
            watching it

ah, look, that muscular youth
      kneels braced on the low mountain
and has pierced the instep of Cassiopeia
         with an arrow.

The vegetarian dog

Though born without malice,
he has an itchy finger,

moves on tiptoes
through the jungle.

can he help it he wears
the stripes of a hyena

and though vegetarian by choice
his olfactories are lined with fangs?:

on his brow he bears the motto
CAVE CANEM for all to see. . .

sweat dripping from his ears
he goes with sickle and bag,

red suns reflected on his bifocals,
collecting oleander blossoms from the high vines

but stumbles on powdery footprints over stone,
and struck to the core of his brain

with a burst of light and hunger,
drops pith hat and field book

runs through the woods
yelping, nose to ground. . .

sees them in a grove sipping vinegar
from silver teacups,

and unslinging his carbine
now light as a feather,

sprays the crowd
with weightless bullets,

rushes into their midst
with drawn bayonet

catching their skirts in his teeth
as they shake loose and fly away.

Rain

When the rain falls
the little girls cover their ears.
when the rain falls
they run hide their dolls
and sit in the corners
nibbling on soap

as the house grows dark
they feel the spikes in their chests —
they know the dwarfs
are mounting the rooftops;
they hear their mothers
screaming in the trees

they plug up their ears with toadstools,
they eat bitter pecans
to make themselves invisible

but the snails in their heads
strain through their fingers,
their tongues tear at the roots
mimicking the sounds . . . how they
wish they could be bronze trees.

when the rain falls
they listen for the echoes
in the cups of their hands

and when it all goes away
they go out in the grass
to gather worms with the birds

To kill a tapeworm

The old method was
to half starve the patient
and when the undernourished
      worm came crawling
up the esophagus to see
      what was up
the dexterous surgeon
      would ZIP
nip off its head which
      killed the worm all right
(except that forever after
      the patient wakes up nights
screaming at the appalling
      taste in his mouth
of the worm's ghost crawling
      up his soul's esophagus)
but which proves nothing except
that tapeworms too get hungry

the best method
which compassionate physicians
never had hoped for
until the advent of the atom bomb
      is to
feed the patient poison
which shocks both the parasite
      and the host
in every respect out of existence
which proves nothing of course
      except
that the only way to completely
      kill a worm is
to burn the apple

Ollas

In the olla
is the form of a snake
and burnt cypress.

the shadow of wings
against the hills.

a procession of cardinals
sucking charcoal
winds across the beaten landscape
to their millennium

a fine down covers the earth

while in her mouth
whirl the dark maps
of serpentine and smokeless worlds.

Consuelo, the north wind
is carrying away your clothes

Consuelo
Consuelo
the north wind is carrying away your clothes
run and take them from the line
run and take them down
before they all blow away

look.
can't you see?
they are all blowing away:
are you blind
like beggars in the market?

the sheets are billowing
like bursting sails
the shirts are flapping
like wounded crows
the pants are frenzied
with the wind and fly out
parallel to the ground.
the handkerchiefs are borne
away like sparrows in a hurricane
and look, the underwear is
shamelessly scattered all over
the neighbor's field

but Consuelo is sleeping
a beautiful sleep
and in her sleeping
dreams of things
the north wind
could never know

she is a pilgrim lost
in a spiritual trance

a beautiful child
sleepwalking in her lovely dreams

why should we waken her now?
it might frighten her
or cause her to panic
and surely it would destroy
her lovely dreams

which the north wind
could never know

which the north wind
could never know

The magic rabbit

No cloak

but long ribbed ears
and thistle balls
                in his eyes.

he talks to the midnight flowers
and they move their arms in assent,

a necklace of wounds
opens at their throat.

the fat boy rides a melon
across the moon
on his way
to the thatched hut of his mother.

News from a New Mexican Village

The outline of Ramon's horse keeps appearing
on the adobe wall, galloping through clouds
and up to his chest in mud. the sky

is intensely free of birds. geese fill the streets,
and a couple of women stagger beneath the shadows
of their loads of wood.

sweat trickles down the back of my neck.
some Indians squat outside the bar, drinking beer
from cans, sinking back into the earth

disguised as a girl, I cross the five rivers
of fire and blood, splinters, saws, and knives,
and crossing the last one,
            throw my comb back into his face:
I go hand in hand through the forest
            with John the Bear.

they move across the yellow street and slouch
in the stark shadow of the wall;
            schoolboys, forgotten
how to take their own scalps,
            dreaming of bulbous cattle.

tomorrow I will take a boy up into
            the mountains
and catch the white,
            cartilaginous horses
that run wild over the rocky canyons.
tomorrow, I will chase away the flies.

Jays

When my father was building a house
in the woods
        nearby our house
for Mr. Wolf,
                I could hear his hammer
through the trees, and the bluejays
were all the time flying
        because of it.

and at lunch time, he worked so close
that I could walk through
              the pine grove
where we had our picnics on holidays,
and hidden in thickets
call him with our secret Indian whistle,
cunningly imitative of birds

and he'd come home through the woods
and we'd sit in our boots eating
slabs of bread and butter with our tea . . .
and all afternoon as I lay in bed
waiting for the masts of ships
      to appear over the spikes of the pines,
I could hear him hammering, hammering. . .

Whales

Behold
    the tracks of whales
        in the sky
discreet as those the dinosaurs
    left frozen in mud
which you can knock your knuckles
        upon.

where they went
   dragging their huge genitals
up through the stars.
and often stopped on ledges
     to rest
or think maybe to cut them off.

but catching their breath
     struggled on
up. up.
      so that now some stars
twinkled beneath them.
until they reached that weightless land,
      entirely silver . . .

see the dark grooves
    they left in the heavens.

The Angels of San Simon

The angels of San Simon
        stand still as gas pumps
and leave no footprints in the sand;
leaning against the houses,
           all week long
they clean their nails
        or squint, slouching, out across the chaparral,
           gnawing their fingers to the bone;
the clapboards of the town
        are scrawled with their faint images.

for diversion
        they stir the dust
           into housewives' milk,

or unseen by cats
        delve into apple barrels
           and pit the skins;

with thin hands
        they squeeze the cowboys
           by their testicles.

they touch the yellow cows
        and bring the ague
           and fever in . . .

and on Sunday afternoons fly out
to the stagnant air pooled
above the mountains, blowing their paper
horns into the stifled sky,
etching oxidized horizons
with the brittle streamers
of their fine wasted hair;

making the rounds
circle back
and land, scarcely breathing,
and stand still
as gas pumps,
leaving hardly a footprint
in the sand.

Balcony

after sunset
the streets
        are full
of children
        laughing through the trees.

in the first long
                twilight
after winter,
        in dark stairways
and around the corners of buildings

they rustle
        with children
coming
        like smoke
                unwinding . . .

in the first warm
                colored hours
they know it in their bones
        and in their pockets,

and they are off in the parks
        and in the hedges
        and across the soggy grass,
        almost like Indians . . .

they rustle
        with children
coming
        like smoke
                unwinding;

and the streets
        are clean
and empty.

Upon approaching the village

And when they ask us
                tell them
a band of robbers came leaping
over the moonlit boulders;
slaughtered our servants,
demanded to know
where the gold was. took
everything but our lives:

among these clods
it is better to be known
as fallen kings than as beggars.

The Palace at 4 a.m.

Mother,
    I am going home.

through the great transparent
                        ear
    hanging
        tense in darkness.

overhead
    an antediluvian bird
        with hollow bones
        (made for flutes)
    rakes the sky
        with its teeth.

my heart is made of an apple
        instantly full-blown
    and ready to be cut:
I have watched
    the digital afternoons
        blow away
        like pieces of smouldering straw
    into an amputated sky,
        which ignores them . . .

I want my bath now,
    of raw ambergris
    and charred cloves.

and stroke my sister's chilly backbone,
                    picked clean of meat,
          while I watch them take her head away
          in a basket of brown roses.

in the roofless attic
          an antediluvian bird
                    rakes the stars,
                    like plankton,
                         through its teeth.

Mother, I want to be born.

and a massive hound
          bearing a stomach of coals in his mouth
                    knocks on the door
          with his wooden head.

*This book was composed in Trump Mediaeval italic
and bold type designed by Georg Trump and produced
by the C. E. Weber Typefoundry of Stuttgart, Germany.
It was set by Craftsman Type, Dayton, Ohio. The offset
lithography is by Young & Klein Inc., and the book-
binding is by Cincinnati Bindery, both of Cincinnati.
Camerata XII text and cover papers are from
Nationwide Papers Incorporated, Chicago, Illinois.*